THIS BOOK BELONGS TO:

_____

AXOLOTL LOVE

Mimi Jones

Dedicated to all the axolotl lovers.

ISBN 978-1-958985-28-1

www.joeysavestheday.com

A Mimi Book

I love you a whole lotl!

An axolotl enjoying a smoothie like a genuine aquatic connoisseur!

Smile

A grinning axolotl flashing you a cheeky smile!

An axolotl gliding through the water like a tiny aquatic superstar!

A groovin' and shakin' axolotl, belting out tunes and busting moves!

Axolotl donut party, here we come!

Axolotl dives into some iPad shenanigans!

Splish-splash shenanigans for the axolotl!

Oh la la, it's axolotl noodle love!

Adorable pumpkin axolotl extravaganza!

Yummy ice cream galore!

Fry me a river, because I'm all
about those golden crispy delights!

Big squishy axolotl cuddles!

6+2=8

Axolotl mastering the art of adding!

Lights, camera, axolotl action!

AWESOME

Have an axolotl-ly awesome day!

Axolotl fiesta floaties!

HAPPY

An axolotl doing the happy swim!

Lotl slurpy noodles!

AHOY!

Ahoy, matey! It's a swashbuckling axolotl ready to sail the seven seas!

A giant, squishy wave from your adorable little axolotl buddy!

Cupid the axolotl is here, sprinkling love like it's confetti!

A delightful basket overflowing with axolotl affection!

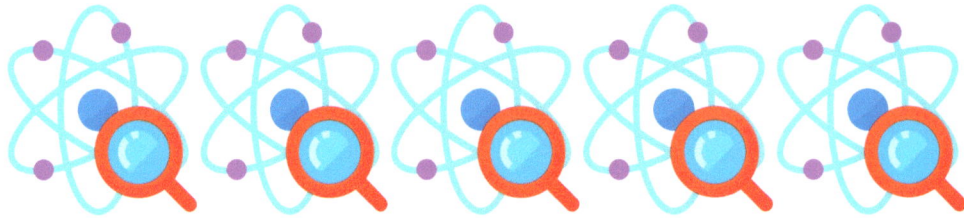

It's science o'clock, and this axolotl is ready to get its geek on!

A whole lotl unicorn love!

An axolotl dreaming of a harmonious planet!

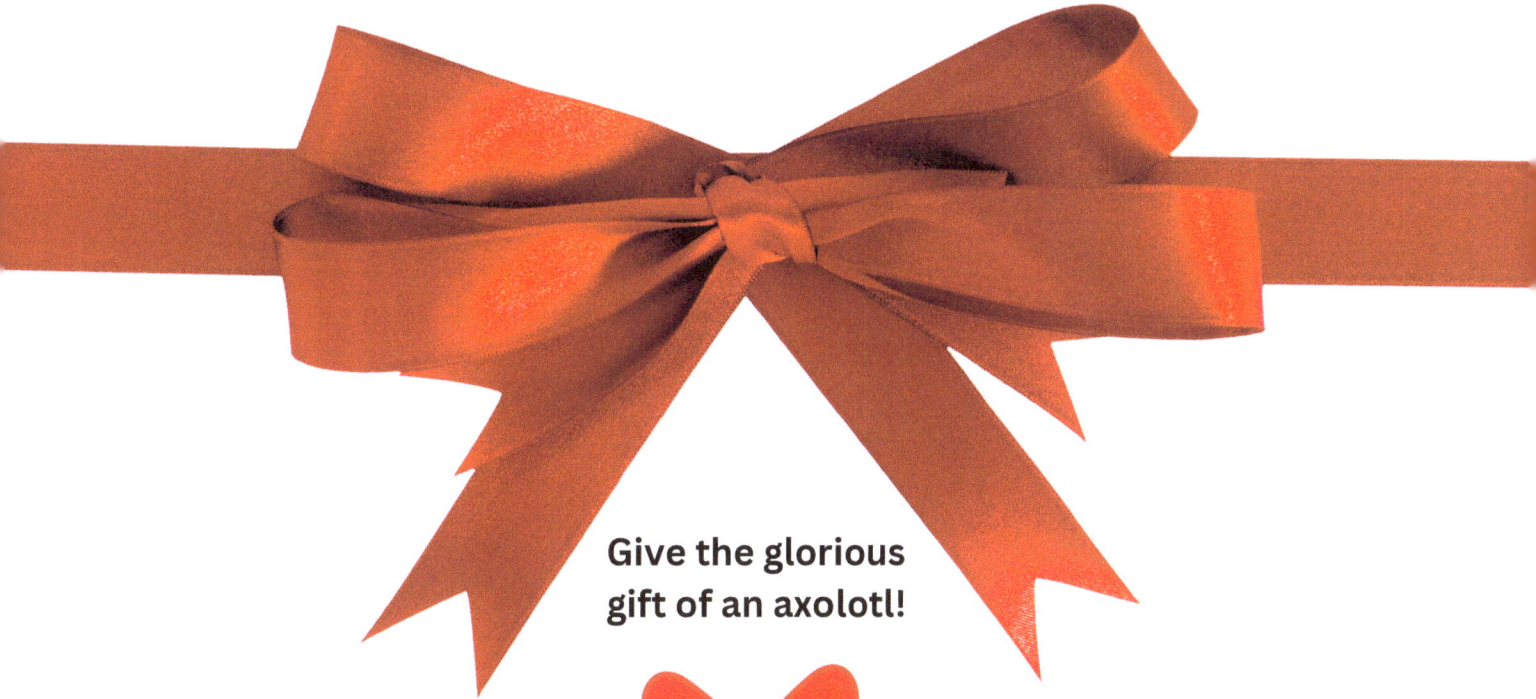

Give the glorious
gift of an axolotl!

sweet dreams

A tiny, snoozy axolotl!

This adorable axolotl is here to sprinkle some sweet dream magic your way!

This is a whimsical, adorable, and giggle-inducing book! Fun fact: Axolotls actually chill out in calm lakes or cozy fish tanks!

GOOD BYE!

www.ingramcontent.com/pod-product-compliance
Lightning Source LLC
Chambersburg PA
CBHW060836270326
41933CB00002B/104